July 26, 2025

Dear Eleanore,

What a fun time we had in Paris! I'll always remember a lovely day with you, Beatrice + George at the David Hockney exhibit and the amusement park! And how fun that you could have a sleep~~over~~ "under" with George! I hope you weren't too tired today!

Love,
Caroline

Casterman
Rue Haute 139
1000 Bruxelles
Belgique

www.casterman.com

ISBN: 978-2-203-28601-6
Edition number: L.10EJCN000737.N001

Text by Rosalind Elland-Goldsmith
Translated into English by Chloë Prestwich
Layout by Neil Desmet

Cover: Vladimir Sazonov/Adobe Stock ; page 5: Boraryn/Adobe Stock ; page 6: Jérôme Delaunay/IStock ; page 7: Alexander Demyanenko/Adobe Stock ; pages 8, 9, 10, 11, 12, 13, 14, 15, 17, 18, 19, 21 et 23: Neil Desmet ; page 16: saiko3p/Adobe Stock ; page 20: Arthur Weidmann/Wikimediacommons [https://creativecommons.org/licenses/by-sa/4.0/deed.fr] ; page 22: olrat/Adobe Stock ; page 24: Lamiot/Wikimediacommons [https://creativecommons.org/licenses/by-sa/4.0/deed.en] and Neil Desmet ; page 25: Rostislav Glinsky/Adobe Stock ; page 26: Ekaterina Belova/Adobe Stock.

Based on Gilbert Delahaye and Marcel Marlier's picture books. The illustrations are taken and adapted from *Martine à la maison, Martine au zoo, Martine - Les quatre saisons, Martine en bateau, Martine fait du camping* and *Martine prend l'avion.*

Printed in January 2024, in France, by PPO Graphic (10 rue de la Croix Martre, 91120 Palaiseau).
Legal deposit: March 2024 ; D.2024/0053/162
Deposited at the Ministry of Justice, Paris (law n°49.956 of July 16, 1949, on publications aimed at young people)

MADE IN FRANCE

Gilbert Delahaye ◆ Marcel Marlier

martine

visits Paris

casterman

The holidays have finally arrived! Martine and Jean are thrilled: they're going to spend a few days at their auntie Flo and uncle Max's house… in Paris!

"Flo will take you to the Natural History Museum, where she works," Martine's mum announces as they arrive on the Avenue des Champs-Élysées after a several hour drive.

"It's an amazing place to find out about animals and extinct species."

"Extinct species?" Martine repeats, surprised.

"Yes, most of them had so many predators, including humans, that they eventually died. They no longer exist today."

"I hope that never happens to dogs…" Martine whispers, stroking Patapouf, who doesn't seem a bit worried!

"Hi Flo!" Martine and Jean shout as they arrive on the top floor of a beautiful stone building. "We've brought you some daffodils from our garden."

"Oh, thank you! I'm delighted to welcome you to Paris," the young woman exclaims. "See what a beautiful city it is! And I've thought of a fun way for you to visit its various districts. Starting tomorrow, you'll go on a treasure hunt looking for seven animals, scattered across the city. If you find them all, you'll win a big surprise!"

Martine and Jean are very excited. They can't wait to start the game!

The following day, once their parents have left, Flo takes her niece and nephew to Montmartre.

"The Sacré-Cœur Basilica offers a breathtaking view of the capital," she says, facing the panorama.

"What a gigantic city..." Jean whispers, bewildered.

"And it's also beautiful!" Martine adds.

"This is where the game begins," Flo announces, pulling out from her bag a small sheet of paper, folded in four.

"Here is the first clue: 'My name means to constantly remind or criticise someone. My hair is called a mane...'"

"What could it be?" Martine and Jean rack their brains while they walk down the steps of the Sacré-Cœur.

"I know!" Martine suddenly shouts, with a tap on her forehead. "Nag… which means…"

"A horse!" Jean answers. "But where can we find a horse in Montmartre?"

"Right there!" Martine exclaims with a big smile, pointing at the colourful animals on the Saint-Pierre merry-go-round.

"Well done!" Flo congratulates. "And since we're here, who would like to go for a ride?"

As she climbs on the wooden horse's back, Martine notices a piece of paper wedged under its saddle.

"Jean, look… it's a new clue!"

This time, her brother reads it:

"'I am as blue as the waters of the Nile. I am waiting for you in the former residence of the kings of France.'"

"'The former residence of the kings of France…' That could mean the Louvre!" Martine suggests. "I visited it with my class. But the Louvre is a huge place… I'm worried we won't find what we're looking for."

"The clue also mentions the Nile, which is a river in Egypt..." Jean points out.

"Right! Then, we must go to the Department of Egyptian Antiquities," Martine works out.

As soon as they step inside the famous museum, the two children follow the signs that lead to the collections of ancient art. As they walk through one of the galleries, Martine spots a little blue china hippopotamus.

"Blue as the waters of the Nile," she recites, beaming. "We've found the second animal!"

"You're very clever!" Flo admits, smiling.

Flo invites the children to walk across the Pont des Arts when a stranger stops them.

"I am a friend of your aunt's, and I have something for you..." she explains with a wink, handing them a piece of paper.

"'You will find the next animal by the water,'" Martine reads.

"Right now, we're standing above the water..." Jean thinks out loud. "Maybe we should walk down to the riverside?"

"OK," Martine agrees. "But watch out for Patapouf, there are so many boats navigating the Seine!"

The three of them walk down the steps leading to the bank.

"I can't see anything…" the little girl whispers, sitting down on the cobblestones. "The clue is a bit vague."

"There's nothing but passers-by and swans…" Jean sighs.

"Did you say swans?" Martine cries. "That must be it!" They look up towards the Pont des Arts where Flo is watching them and point to the beautiful white bird. The young woman nods and gives a thumbs up to congratulate them.

From the Pont des Arts, Martine and Jean can see the Musée d'Orsay.

"That's where the most beautiful Impressionist paintings are exibited…" Flo explains. "Pictures by great painters, such as Monet, Renoir and Cézanne. But Orsay wasn't always a museum."

"Was it a factory?" Jean asks.

His aunt shakes her head and points at the building's façade. "It bears a big clock, similar to the ones you always see in..."

"… Train stations!" Martine cries. "Orsay was a train station!"

"Yes!" Flo agrees. "Now, let's go home. You've been very observant today."

As soon as they wake up the following day, Martine and Jean get ready to follow Flo to Île Saint-Louis.

"This island is packed with beautiful houses and 'bouquinistes', that sell second-hand books," their aunt explains. "You can also enjoy delicious ice creams on Île Saint-Louis. Who fancies one?"

Martine and Jean both raise their hands. But, what a surprise! When Martine opens her purse to pay for her brother and her aunt, she finds a piece of paper folded in four. The fourth clue, of course!

"'From the top of the cathedral, we are the fantastic beasts that keep a close eye on the capital.'" Jean reads.

The children are intrigued.

"Is there a cathedral in the area?" Martine asks the ice cream man.

"Only the most famous one of them all!" he says. "Notre-Dame de Paris!" Martine, Jean and Patapouf run to the paved square of the cathedral and scan the façade. Several monstrous figures are carved in the stone.

"You do have a sharp eye!" Flo applauds. "Those are called gargoyles. They are said to protect Notre-Dame against demons…"

"This is a very old neighbourhood, isn't it?" Martine asks, as the three of them stroll around.

"One of the oldest," Flo confirms. "However, in Paris there are surprises on every street corner..."

No sooner have they crossed the Seine that they come across a large square overlooked by a futuristic and colourful building.

"That's the Pompidou Centre, which also goes by the name Beaubourg!"

"It looks like the pipes and the escalator were built on the outside," Jean points out. "Shall we go up?"

But Patapouf pulls on his lead. Never will he enter the strange tunnel which stretches up to the sky!

Martine kneels down to comfort him… and notices a piece of paper stuck under his collar.

"Well now, Patapouf!" she laughs. "You're the one carrying the clue!" This time, the clue is neither a riddle nor a brainteaser, just three words: "Sssssstick with me."

Confused, Martine and Jean start looking around again. They wander around the Pompidou Centre and spot the Stravinsky Fountain. Several statues emerge from the water, including a sculpture of…

"A snake!" Martine exclaims. "That's five!"

"It's time for lunch. I'm taking you to Place des Vosges," Flo announces. "We'll meet Max there. He works in the area."

Twenty minutes later, they all settle on the lawn in a big green square lined with arches and brick buildings.

"Many artists have lived here," Max explains while handing out sandwiches. "Including the famous writer, Victor Hugo!"

For the rest of the day, Flo, her nephew, and her niece visit the Marais district before they hop onto a bus at Place de la Bastille.

"Can you believe this is where the French Revolution started?" Martine whispers to her brother.

ıe evening, disaster strikes… Jean has a fever!

'Maybe you caught a cold during the picnic," Flo suggests. "Best you stay at home with Max tomorrow.

"OK…" Jean sighs, disappointed that he won't carry on with the treasure hunt. "Martine, I'm counting on you to find the remaining clues."

"Of course, plus I won't be alone… I have Patapouf!"

Before entering the metro with Flo the next morning, Martine says to Patapouf:

"We're going underground. But don't be scared. Mum told me that Parisians have been taking the metro for over a century. Everything will be fine!"

When they exit the metro, Flo takes Martine to the Jardin de Luxembourg. At the gates, she hands her some money as well as a new clue.

"A riddle! 'My neck is white, my head emerald green, and I have webbed feet.'"

"Let's meet back here in an hour, Martine," Flo says.

As she admires the park's pathways lined with green chairs, Martine wonders: "I know the answer to the riddle… but where will I find ducks in the middle of Paris?"

Just then, Patapouf takes off towards a glistening pond. Little remote-controlled boats sail in the sun among seagulls and… ducks! That's animal number six!

"Thanks, Patapouf. You helped me find the second to last animal!" Martine cries. "As a reward, I'm taking you to the swings."
But when they arrive, the ticket seller hands Martine a very familiar-looking piece of paper, which says: "I'm the last animal on the list – a sleeping and extinct animal."
After a go on the swings, Martine sits on a chair to figure out the clue. An extinct animal… That reminds her of the conversation she had in the car with her mother. "Extinct species are on display at the museum where Flo works!" she remembers as she runs off to find her aunt.

Half an hour later, as they enter the Natural History Museum, Flo says to her niece:

"You can walk around the Gallery of Evolution. Once you've found the last animal, come and find me in my office."

Martine admires the dinosaur fossils and sea animal skeletons. On the second floor, she sees a sign pointing to the "Room of endangered and extinct species."

Martine approaches a strange looking bird. It has a hooked beak, small wings, and stocky feet… Martine has never seen anything like it. She bends down to read the name on the plaque and laughs:

"It's a dodo! That's why the clue mentioned the animal was asleep…" Hurray! Martine has completed the treasure hunt! She runs off to see her aunt.

"Well done, Martine!" Flo says. "Let's go home and share the good news with Jean. Tomorrow, I'll reveal the big surprise… the highlight of the capital!"

The following day, Jean is much better.

"I wonder what Flo wants to show us," he whispers to his sister as they catch the bus to La Sorbonne, the oldest university in Paris. Martine has an idea but she keeps quiet. She wouldn't want to spoil the surprise!

After a day wandering around the Latin Quarter, the children head to a square called Le Parvis des Droits de l'Homme. They cannot believe their eyes when they arrive. Because in front of them stands…

The Eiffel Tower!

"The most spectacular and most famous monument in Paris," Flo announces, with a grin.

Martine and Jean remain speechless. They gaze at the Iron Lady which stands out against the setting sun.

"Time for a photo!" Flo says, as she comes back from a balloon stand. "Say cheese, Martine, Jean… even you, Patapouf! Then, we'll go up to the top of the tower - that will be your prize for completing the treasure hunt which lead you through the beautiful city of Paris!"

Martine's Journey Through Paris

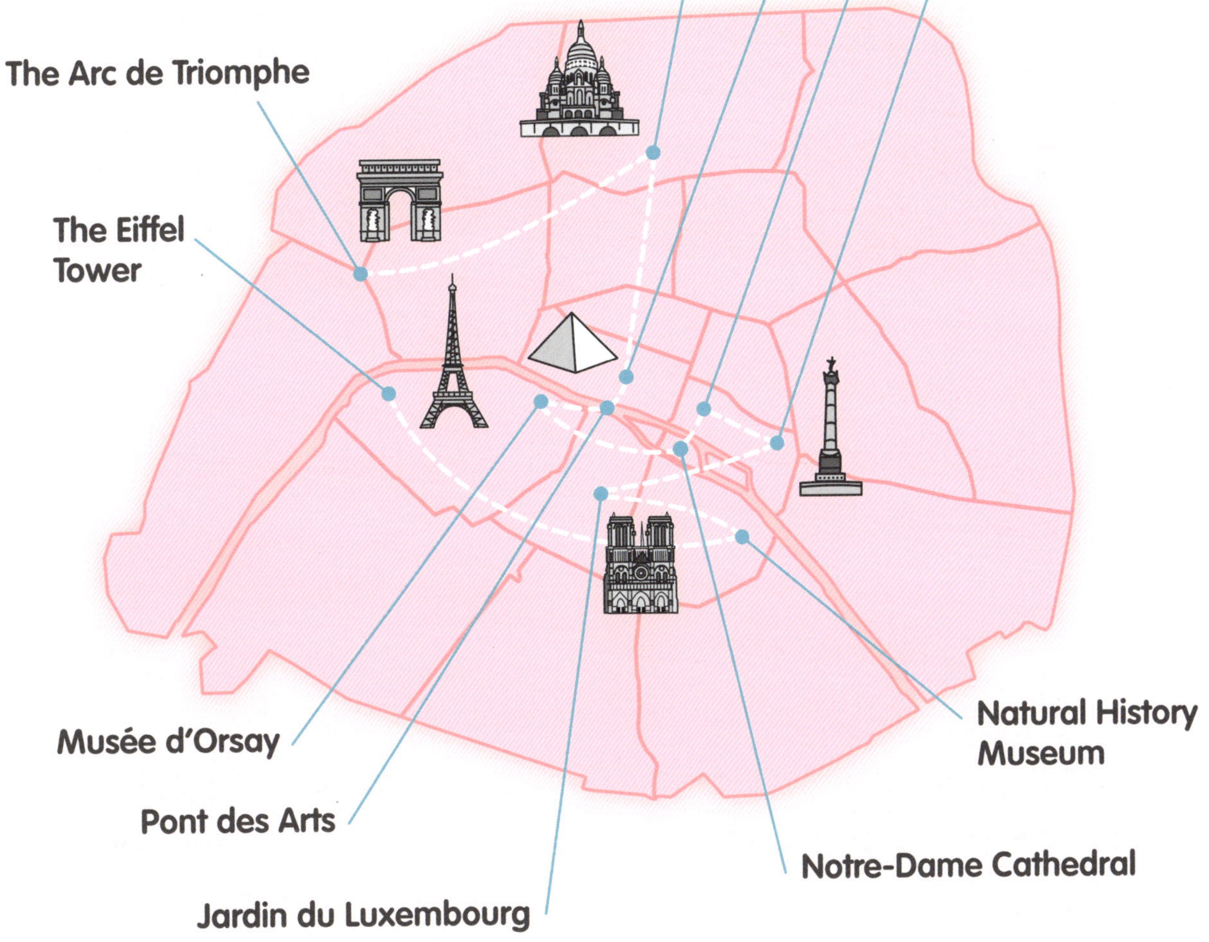

Paris' Major Monuments

The Arc de Triomphe

Under this arch overlooking the Avenue des Champs-Élysées is the Flame of Remembrance. It is positioned in front of the Tomb of the Unknown Soldier and pays tribute to all the soldiers who died for France.

Sacré-Cœur

222... That's the number of steps on Montmartre hill that you must climb to reach the foot of this basilica. Otherwise, you can always use the funicular!

The Louvre

Before becoming the most visited museum in the world, the Louvre was a fortress. It then became a palace where several kings lived. 33,000 works of art are now exhibited there... Truly magnificent!

Musée d'Orsay

The beautifully restored clocks are evidence that the museum used to be a train station. Nowadays it houses one of the world's largest collections of Impressionist art!

Notre-Dame de Paris

Even though Victor Hugo's novel "Notre-Dame de Paris" made it famous, the cathedral was hated for a long time. Since the terrible fire in 2019, over a hundred craftsmen and labourers work on it's restoration every day.

The Pompidou Centre

This museum, also known as "Beaubourg," has a distinctive architectural design. The colours of the exterior pipes were not chosen randomly: each is linked to one of the building's functions. Blue symbolizes air circulation; yellow, electricity; green, water... Interesting, isn't it?

Natural History Museum

An extinct dodo, a narwhal with a huge tusk, a giant tortoise... these are only a few of the 300,000 species on display in the museum's Gallery of Evolution. To observe them is to better understand where humans come from and the history of mankind.

The Eiffel Tower

Built for the 1889 Universal Exhibition, for its time the Eiffel Tower was a true feat of engineering. Standing 300 metres high, it was built in record time (in just two years and two months!), and visitors could take elevators to the top. Never before had such a height been reached!